Filipino Favorites

Norma Olizon-Chikiamco

PERIPLUS

Glossary

Ampalaya, also known as bitter melon, is a cylindrical, wrinkled, green "melon" which has a distinctive bitter taste. It is available from Filipino grocers.

Annatto seeds are known as *atsuete* in Tagalog. These dried, dark reddish-brown seeds are often used as food coloring or dye. The seeds are soaked, then squeezed in water to extract the red coloring, which lends an orange to reddish tint to food.

Beancurd is known as *tokwa* in Tagalog. Rich in protein, beancurd can be steamed or deep-fried, pickled or fermented. Soft white *tokwa* is steamed or added to soups; hard squares of *tokwa* are deep-fried; small cubes of dried beancurd are added to slow-cooked dishes. Red or white fermented *tokwa*, sold in jars, is used as a seasoning.

Capsicum, also known as bell peppers, are often used in fresh salads and Spanish-style dishes or stews.

Chilies come in two basic varieties, the small and very hot chilies called *siling labuyo*, which are often chopped and used in dipping sauces; and the long flat finger-length cooking pepper called *siling mahaba*, often cooked with soups like *sinigang* or *paksiw*. Hot chilies are used sparingly—with the amount of heat increasing as the size diminishes, and as the color matures toward red. To reduce the heat of a chili while retaining the flavor, remove the seeds.

Chorizo sausages are any dried Spanish-style pork sausage packed in paprika-flavored lard. Used for flavoring dishes such as *cocido* or *pochero*, it is usually added to stews, rather than eaten on its own. Widely available from Filipino (and European) supermarkets.

Coconut is widely used in Asian cooking. Fresh young coconut (*buko*) provides a refreshing juice and sweet white flesh. A mature coconut (*niyog*) is grated, then squeezed in water to make coconut milk (*gata*). Coconut milk is the basis of the creamy-hot recipes of the Bicol region. Canned coconut milk is available wherever Asian food is sold. Skim off the thicker solids from the top of the cans for "coconut cream". Coconut oil is extracted from long-simmered coconut milk during the preparation of *latik*, a brown granular residue that is used as a topping for some desserts.

Cornflour or cornstarch is a fine white powder often used as a thickening agent. It does not add much fat or change the flavor of a dish.

Eggplant, known as *talong* in Tagalog, is of the slender purple-skinned variety.

Talong is usually grilled over the stove before being chopped and made into a salad; or stuffed (*Rellenong Talong*); or sautéed in a vegetable dish like Pinakbet.

Fish paste is known as *bagoong* in Tagalog. This salty, fermented paste is used as a sauce accompaniment to many meals. If unavailable, substitute Indonesian *trassi*, Malaysian *belacan* or Thai *kapi*. Local fish paste comes in two main varieties: *bagoong alamang*—a paste made of tiny shrimp; and *bagoong* Balayan—a thick fermented liquid paste from Balayan, Batangas.

Kangkong is a deep-green aquatic plant with heart-shaped leaves, popular throughout Southeast Asia. Also known as water convolvulus and sometimes water spinach or swamp cabbage, it is full of nutrition and possesses an excellent flavor. *Kangkong* is sautéed with garlic or mixed into *sinigang*.

Lime or *dayap* is about the size of a small egg, with a greenish-yellow skin and tart flavor; it is squeezed for fresh juice or mixed into sauces. The more popular "native lime" is *calamansi*—a small walnut-sized green to yellow-green fruit with an aromatic citrus flavor. *Calamansi* makes a delicious fresh juice and adds its lively accent to many foods, from noodles to desserts.

Noodles can be made from rice or wheat flour or mung beans. Among Filipinos, the most popular varieties are *kanton*, thick, round, yellow fresh egg noodles; *bihon*, dried rice vermicelli; and *sotanghon*, transparent mung-bean noodles, also known as cellophane or glass noodles. *Pancit* is a generic term used to refer to a noodle dish.

Pan de sal is the national bread of the Philippines, which is shaped like a bun. Substitute any bread of your choice.

Patis is a thin fish sauce made from boiled, salted and fermented fish or shrimp. It is used to flavor many dishes. An essential item to have on hand but, if unavailable, substitute Thai *nam pla* or Vietnamese *nuoc mam*.

Spring onion is also known as scallion. This popular green young onion is used as a flavoring in soups and a garnish on meat dishes.

Spring roll wrapper is a thin crêpe made from a batter of rice flour, water and salt. The *lumpia* wrapper is steamed and dried in the sun, then used to wrap a variety of spring rolls. The rice wrapper must be moistened with a wet cloth before using, for greater flexibility.

Vinegar, also known as *suka* or native vinegar, comes in black, red and white hues. It is made from *nipa* palm, coconut, *kaong* or sago palm, as well as from sugar cane. White vinegar can be used for the recipes in this book.

Papaya Achara (Papaya Relish)

2 small unripe papaya, about 500 g (1 lb) each
Coarse salt
300 g (1¹/₂ cups) sugar
375 ml (1¹/₂ cups) white vinegar
¹/₂ teaspoon salt
1 medium carrot, cut into 1-cm (¹/₂-in) slices
1 red capsicum, cut into thin strips
1 green capsicum, cut into thin strips
5 slices ginger
45 g (¹/₂ cup) raisins

Syrup
300 g (1¹/₂ cups) sugar
250 ml (1 cup) cane or white vinegar
1 teaspoon salt

1 Peel papaya then grate flesh into thin strips. Mash the papaya strips with coarse salt. Rinse and squeeze out as much liquid as you can. Pat dry with paper towels.
2 In a large saucepan, mix together sugar, vinegar and salt. Add the papaya and simmer for about 5 minutes. Add carrot and capsicum and simmer for about 5 minutes until carrot is tender . Drain and arrange in a bowl.
3 Soak the ginger in hot water and drain. Toss ginger and raisins with the cooked vegetables.
4 To make the Syrup, combine ingredients in a saucepan. Bring to the boil, lower heat and simmer for 5 minutes.
5 Pour the Syrup on the cooked vegetable, ginger and raisin mixture.
6 Let cool, transfer to a clean container and cover. Store in refrigerator. Serve as relish for roasted or fried meats.

Serves 6
Preparation time: 30 mins
Cooking time: 20 mins

Bagoong Guisado (Shrimp Paste Dip)

2 tablespoons oil
4–5 cloves garlic, peeled and finely chopped
³/₄ cup *bagoong* (shrimp paste)
1 teaspoon white refined sugar
2 tablespoons cane (or cider) vinegar
1–2 *siling labuyo* (finger chilies), cut into ¹/₂ cm (¹/₄ in) pieces (optional)

1 Heat oil in a frying pan for about 1 minute. Sauté garlic until fragrant but not brown. Add *bagoong* and stir-fry for about 1 to 2 minutes.
2 Add sugar and stir until mixture is smooth. Turn off heat.
3 Blend in vinegar and add the chilies if desired. The chilies add spiciness to the *bagoong*. Serve with *Kare-kare*, *Pinakbet* and as a condiment for most rice meals.

Makes 1 cup
Preparation time: **10 mins**
Cooking time: **25 mins**

Lumpiang Sariwa
(Fresh Vegetable Spring Rolls)

2 tablespoons oil
200 g (1 cup) bean curd
100 g (3 oz) string beans, cut diagonally into 2 cm (1 in) pieces
1 medium carrot, cut into thin strips
100 g (³/₄ cup) shredded white cabbage
Salt and pepper
12 spring roll wrappers, steamed
12 lettuce leaves
130 g (1 cup) cooked chickpeas

Brown Sauce
200 g (1 cup) brown sugar
500 ml (2 cups) water
1 teaspoon salt
2 tablespoons soy sauce
2 tablespoons cornstarch
60 ml (¹/₄ cup) water
¹/₂ head of garlic, cloves peeled and crushed

1 To prepare Brown Sauce, blend sugar, water, salt and soy sauce, bring to the boil then simmer 5 minutes. In a small bowl, blend cornstarch with the water until smooth. Stir into the saucepan. Simmer until mixture thickens, about 10 to 15 minutes.
2 Heat oil in a pan and fry bean curd. Remove from pan and cut into narrow strips. Set aside.
3 Blanch the string beans, carrot strips and cabbage by plunging in boiling water for about 5 minutes. Drain immediately and plunge into a bowl of iced water. Drain well then season with salt and pepper.
4 Steam a spring roll wrapper for about 5 minutes. Line a wrapper with a lettuce leaf. Spoon 2 to 3 tablespoons of the blanched vegetables onto the lettuce leaf. Add about 1 tablespoon of the chickpeas and the cooked bean curd. Roll wrapper and tuck in the ends to seal completely. Repeat with remaining vegetables and wrappers. Serve with Brown Sauce and crushed garlic.

Serves 4
Preparation time: **40 mins**
Cooking time: **30 mins**

Steam spring roll wrappers to soften.

Line a spring roll with a lettuce leaf.

Spoon the vegetables onto the lettuce leaf.

Roll the leaf and tuck in the ends to seal.

Molo Soup (Wonton Soup)

This dish is a speciality of the Visayas region of the Philippines. The secret to this dish is a good, tasty broth which forms the base of the soup. Preparation can be lengthy so allow ample time to cook and prepare it before serving.

- 500 g (3 cups) ground pork
- 100 g (3/4 cup) canned water chestnuts, finely chopped
- 250 g (4 oz) small prawns, peeled
- 50 g (1/4 cup) finely chopped spring onions (scallions)
- 1 egg
- 2 tablespoons soy sauce
- 1 pack wonton wrappers
- 2 tablespoons oil
- 1 medium onion, finely chopped
- 3–4 cloves garlic, finely chopped
- 2 liters (8 cups) chicken broth
- 250 g (8 oz) chicken breast fillet, sliced into strips
- 2 teaspoons *patis* (fish sauce)

1 In a mixing bowl, combine ground pork and water chestnuts. Chop half of the prawns coarsely and add to the bowl (set aside remaining prawns). Mix in half of the spring onions, the egg and soy sauce.

2 Spread wonton wrappers on a clean work surface and fill each one with about 1 tablespoon of the pork mixture. Brush the edges of the wrappers with a little water and press edges together to seal. Set aside.

3 Heat oil in a casserole. Sauté onion until transparent, then add garlic and sauté until fragrant. Pour in chicken broth and bring to the boil, then drop in the filled wonton wrappers. Simmer 10 to 15 minutes.

4 Add the chicken and continue simmering until chicken and pork mixture are completely cooked. Stir in the reserved prawns. Simmer until prawns are fully cooked. Season with *patis* and garnish with remaining spring onions.

Serves 8
Preparation time: **45 mins**
Cooking time: **45 mins**

Fill each wrapper with 1 tablespoon of the pork mixture.

Press the edges together to seal.

Arroz Caldo (Chicken and Rice Porridge)

A rice porridge rich with the flavors of chicken broth and ginger, this dish is a favorite on cold, rainy nights.

60 ml (¹/₄ cup) olive oil
1 kg (2 lb) chicken, cut
   into serving pieces
1 head garlic, cloves
   peeled and crushed
100 g (3 oz) ginger,
   peeled and cut into
   1 cm (¹/₂ in) slices
300 g (1¹/₂ cups)
   uncooked rice
1³/₄–2 liters (7–8 cups)
   chicken broth
3 tablespoons *patis* (fish
   sauce), or to taste
¹/₄ cup chopped spring
   onions, to garnish
6–8 *calamansi*

1 In a casserole, heat 2 tablespoons of the olive oil. Brown the chicken pieces lightly then remove with a slotted spoon and set aside.
2 In the same casserole, sauté half of the garlic until lightly brown. Remove the browned garlic from pan and set aside. Pour in remaining oil. Sauté ginger and remaining garlic.
3 Add the rice and stir to coat the grains with the oil. Pour in the 1³/₄ liters (7 cups) of chicken broth. Add the chicken and *patis*. Allow to simmer until rice and chicken are fully cooked, about 40 minutes. Add more broth (and fish sauce) if necessary. The mixture should have a soupy consistency when fully cooked.
4 Spoon into individual serving bowls and garnish with the browned garlic and spring onions. Serve with *calamansi*.

Serves 6
Preparation time: 10 mins
Cooking time: 35 mins

Paella

Paella originated in Valencia, Spain, where it remains a popular dish. In the Philippines, which was a Spanish colony for 300 years, this rice dish has evolved to suit local tastes and preferences.

500 grams (1 lb) medium clams
250 grams ($^1/_2$ lb) small squid, ink, heads and tentacles removed
60 ml ($^1/_4$ cup) olive oil
2 chorizo sausages, sliced diagonally into $2^1/_2$-cm (1-in) pieces
1 medium onion, minced
1 large tomato, grated
1 teaspoon paprika
Few saffron threads
$1^1/_2$ liters (6 cups) warm chicken broth
600 g (3 cups) white, short grain rice
500 g (1 lb) medium prawns
1 large green capsicum, sliced lengthwise about 1 cm ($^1/_2$ in) across
1 large red capsicum, sliced lengthwise about 1 cm ($^1/_2$ inch) across
2 hard-boiled eggs, peeled and sliced
1–2 lemons, quartered

Serves 6–8
Preparation time: 25 mins
Cooking time: 40 mins

1 Clean clam shells very well. Steam clams until they open. Discard shells that remain close. Set aside steamed clams. Slice squid into 1-cm ($^1/_2$-in) rings. Set aside.
2 In a skillet, heat 2 tablespoons of the olive oil. Cook the chorizo sausages about 2 minutes on each side or until firm. Remove from skillet and set aside.
3 Heat remaining olive oil over medium heat in a large *paellera* or shallow casserole. Sauté onion 1 to 2 minutes. Stir in grated tomato and cook about 2 minutes. Lower heat and add paprika. Cook about 1 minute. Meanwhile dissolve saffron threads in warm broth. Immediately pour in warm broth so paprika does not burn. Bring to a simmer.
4 Stir in rice, making sure rice is evenly distributed throughout the pan. Simmer for about 10 minutes, stirring occasionally. Add prawns. When prawns are cooked, remove from pan and set aside. Continue simmering for another five minutes then add squid rings and capsicums. Remove squid rings as soon as they are cooked, about one minute. Set aside.
5 Allow rice to simmer until liquid has been absorbed and rice is slightly dry. Remove from heat. Top with clams, chorizo, prawns, squid and hard-boiled eggs, if desired. Serve in *paellera* or serving platter with lemon wedges.

Bringhe (Luzon-style Paella)

This rice dish is similar to paella, but simpler. The use of coconut milk instead of a meat broth gives it a tropical touch. This dish is often served in town fiestas.

60 ml ($^1/_4$ cup) oil
250 g ($1^1/_2$ cups) chicken breast fillet or thigh fillet, cut into strips
1 medium onion, finely chopped
3–4 cloves garlic, peeled and diced
200 g (1 cup) regular rice
200 g (1 cup) sticky rice
500 ml (2 cups) water
250 ml (1 cup) coconut milk
2 teaspoons turmeric powder
250 g (8 oz) medium prawns, peeled
100 g (2–3 slices) cooked ham, cut into 2-cm (1-in) squares
100 g ($^3/_4$ cup) frozen green peas, thawed
Salt and pepper

1 Heat half of the oil in a casserole and sauté the chicken strips until cooked. Remove chicken from pan and set aside. Pour in remaining oil and sauté onion until transparent. Add garlic and sauté a further 1 minute. Add both kinds of rice and stir to coat in oil.
2 In a large bowl, blend together water, coconut milk and turmeric powder then pour into casserole. Cover and simmer until rice is done, about 25 to 30 minutes.
3 Meanwhile, in a steamer, steam the prawns until cooked and evenly orange in color. Remove from heat and set aside.
4 When rice is fully cooked, stir in the prawns, the chicken strips, cooked ham and green peas. Season with salt and pepper and serve.

Serves 6–8
Preparation time: **5–10 mins**
Cooking time: **40 mins**

Arroz a la Cubana (Cuban-style Rice)

A complex dish with various flavors, Arroz a la Cubana combines the richness of meat with the sweet tastes of fried bananas and raisins. Eggs fried sunny side up make this a very filling, one-dish meal.

125 ml ($1/2$ cup) corn oil
1 medium potato, peeled and diced
3–4 *saba* bananas (plantains), peeled and halved lengthwise
6–8 whole eggs
1 small onion, finely chopped
4 garlic cloves, peeled, crushed and finely chopped
500 g (3 cups) ground pork
2 teaspoons salt
500 g (3 cups) ground beef
Worcestershire sauce
200 g ($1 1/4$ cups) frozen green peas, thawed
90 g ($1/2$ cup) raisins

Serves 6–8
Preparation time: 10 mins
Cooking time: 30 mins

1 In a wok or skillet, heat 2 tablespoons of the corn oil and sauté the potato until almost tender. Remove from the wok and set aside in a bowl. In the same wok, add another 2 tablespoons oil and reheat. Fry the bananas until light brown and tender. Remove and drain on paper towels and set aside.

2 In a separate pan, heat another 2 tablespoons oil and fry the eggs, sunny side up one or two at a time, adding more oil if necessary. Remove eggs as they cook and set aside.

3 Heat the remaining oil in a large skillet or casserole and sauté onion and garlic. Stir in ground pork and cook until brown. Season with $1/2$ teaspoon of the salt.

4 Stir in ground beef and cook, stirring well with the other ingredients until beef browns. Season with $1/2$ teaspoon salt. Stir in a dash of Worcestershire sauce.

5 Mix in green peas and stir well. Add the cooked potatoes and raisins. Season with remaining salt. Heat through for about 5 minutes.

6 To serve, spoon the ground meat mixture into a serving platter. Arrange cooked eggs and bananas on top and serve with plain rice.

Pancit Palabok (Seafood Noodles)

500 g (1 lb) medium
  prawns
3 liters (12 cups) water
60 ml ($^1/_4$ cup) oil
6 tablespoons finely
  chopped garlic
250 g (1$^1/_2$ cups) diced
  pork
200 g ($^3/_4$ cup) *tokwa*
  (hard beancurd
  squares), cubed
2 tablespoons annatto
  seeds soaked in
  2 tablespoons corn oil
2 tablespoons *patis*
  (fish sauce)
2 tablespoons cornstarch
  dissolved in 60 ml
  ($^1/_4$ cup) water
400 g (11 oz) *bihon*
  noodles (dried rice
  vermicelli), soaked in
  water 5 minutes,
  drained
50 g (2 oz) ground
  chicharon (pork
  crackers)
100 g (3$^1/_2$ oz) spring
  onions (scallions),
  chopped
2 hard-boiled eggs,
  quartered
Calamansi, to garnish

1 Peel prawns, reserving shells and heads. Simmer shells and heads in 500 ml (2 cups) water until water turns orange in color. Strain into a bowl, pressing on the heads and shells to extract the juice. Reserve prawn stock and discard shells. Briefly simmer the peeled prawns in 500 ml (2 cups) fresh water, just until shrimps turn an even orange color. Drain shrimps and set aside as topping.

2 In a wok, heat 2 tablespoons of the oil and sauté garlic until brown. Remove from heat and set aside to garnish.

3 Heat remaining 2 tablespoons cooking oil in a pan and sauté pork until fully cooked. Remove from heat and set aside. In the same pan, sauté the *tokwa* until brown. Set aside.

4 Press the soaking annatto seeds in corn oil to extract color (which should be bright orange). Strain the oil into a bowl and set aside.

5 In a saucepan, simmer the prawn stock, stir in the orange-colored annatto oil and season with *patis*. Stir in the cornstarch mixture and simmer until the liquid thickens, stirring occasionally, about 3 to 5 minutes.

6 Bring the remaining 2 liters (8 cups) of water to the boil in a stockpot. Drop in the noodles and simmer for 5 minutes or until tender. Drain.

7 Arrange noodles on a serving platter. Pour in the prawn stock. Arrange the cooked pork, *tokwa*, prawns and *chicharon* on top. Garnish with the fried garlic, spring onions and pieces of hard-boiled egg. Serve with plenty of *calamansi*.

Serves 6–8 ·
Preparation time: 30 mins
Cooking time: 30 mins

Sotanghon (Chicken and Pork Vermicelli)

250 g (8 oz) *sotanghon* (glass or cellophane) noodles

2 tablespoons oil

1 small onion, chopped

3–4 garlic cloves, crushed

250 g (1$^1/_2$ cups) diced lean pork

250 g (1$^1/_2$ cups) sliced chicken breast or thigh fillet

1 carrot, sliced into 1-cm ($^1/_2$-in) rounds

100 g (3 oz) string beans, cut diagonally into 1-cm ($^1/_2$-in) pieces

$^1/_2$ head medium cabbage, cut into thin strips

5–6 pieces fresh *shiitake* mushrooms, cut into strips (see Note)

750 ml (3 cups) water

2 chicken stock cubes

2 tablespoons soy sauce

2 tablespoons chopped spring onions (scallions), to garnish

3–4 *calamansi*, sliced in half

1 Place the noodles in a bowl of water to soak for 15 minutes. Meanwhile, heat oil in a wok and sauté onion until transparent. Add garlic and sauté until fragrant. Brown the diced pork in same wok, then add the sliced chicken and fry for a further 2 minutes.

2 Stir in the carrot rounds, string beans, cabbage and mushrooms. Cook, stirring to mix ingredients, for about 5 minutes. Pour in the 750 ml (3 cups) water and add the stock cubes.

3 Drain the noodles and, with kitchen scissors, cut into smaller pieces (if desired). Add the noodles to the wok. Season with soy sauce and stir mixture well. Let simmer over low heat for 10 minutes or until most of the liquid has been absorbed.

4 Transfer to a serving platter and garnish with spring onions. Serve with *calamansi*.

If using dried shiitake mushrooms, soak the mushrooms in warm water for about 20 minutes to soften before adding to the dish.

Serves 4–6
Preparation time: **20 mins**
Cooking time: **20–30 mins**

Pinakbet (Vegetable Stew)

A favorite dish in the Ilocos region, this vegetable stew has also become popular in other parts of the Philippines. The trick to cooking *pinakbet* is not to stir the vegetables during the cooking process as this could make the dish bitter. *Bagoong*, fermented shrimp or fish paste, is the main flavoring for this dish.

1 whole *ampalaya* (bitter melon), about 150 g (5 oz), sliced into 4-cm ($1^3/_4$-in) pieces
Coarse salt
125 ml ($^1/_2$ cup) cane (or white) vinegar
200 g ($6^1/_2$ oz) pork *liempo* (belly), cubed
250 ml (1 cup) water
2 tablespoons oil
1 medium onion, sliced diagonally
3 medium tomatoes, sliced diagonally
1 bunch (100 g) *sitaw* (snake beans), cut into 4-cm (2-in) lengths
100 g ($3^1/_2$ oz) ladies' fingers (okra), trimmed and sliced diagonally into 2-cm (1-in) pieces
150 g (5 oz) squash, peeled and cubed
150 g (5 oz) small eggplants, cut diagonally into 1-cm ($^1/_2$-in) slices
$^1/_2$ head garlic, cloves peeled and chopped
$^1/_4$ cup *bagoong* (shrimp paste)

1 Sprinkle salt on *ampalaya* and pour in the vinegar to remove some of its bitter taste. Let rest for about 20 minutes, then drain.

2 Meanwhile, in a saucepan, simmer pork in water for 5 minutes until almost cooked. Remove pork from pan and reserve the stock. Heat oil in a frying-pan and brown the pork. Set aside the pork and reserve the pork oil.

3 Arrange *ampalaya* on the bottom of a large casserole or claypot. Add, in layers, the onion, tomatoes, *sitaw*, ladies' fingers, squash and eggplants. Sprinkle crushed garlic over it, then top with the pork and pour in the reserved pork oil.

4 Combine *bagoong* and the reserved pork stock in a small bowl. Mix well then pour into the casserole or claypot. Let it simmer for 10 minutes or until the vegetables are tender but still crisp.

5 Serve with rice and additional *bagoong* if desired.

Serves 6–8
Preparation time: 20 mins
Cooking time: 10 mins

Dinengdeng
(Stewed Vegetables with Fried Fish)

60 ml (¹/₄ cup) oil
2–4 small fish such as
  hasa-hasa (short
  mackerel), *galunggong*
  (round scad) or tilapia
500 g (1 lb) chayote
  (christophene), cut into
  chunks
300 g (10 oz) eggplants,
  sliced into 1-cm (¹/₂-in)
  pieces
100 g (3¹/₃ oz) *sitaw*,
  (snake beans), sliced
  into 4-cm (2-in) pieces
2 tablespoons *bagoong*
  (shrimp paste)
60 ml (¹/₄ cup) water

1 Heat oil in a frying pan and fry the fish on both sides until fully cooked. Set aside to cool slightly, then slice. In a large saucepan or casserole, arrange the chayote, eggplants, *sitaw* and fish slices.
2 In a small bowl, mix *bagoong* with water until smooth, then pour into the casserole.
3 Simmer over medium heat until vegetables are cooked but still firm.

Serves 4
Preparation time: **5 mins**
Cooking time: **25 mins**

Ensaladang Pinoy
(Green Salad)

Lettuce leaves, torn
3–4 medium tomatoes, quartered
1 medium yellow onion, sliced vertically
1 medium cucumber, peeled and cut in 1-cm ($^1/_2$-in) slices

Dressing
200 g (1 cup) caster sugar
750 ml (1$^1/_2$ cups) white or cider vinegar
1 teaspoon salt
1 tablespoon *patis* (fish sauce)
Freshly ground black pepper

1 In a salad bowl, toss together lettuce, tomatoes, onion and cucumber.
2 Make the dressing by combining sugar, vinegar, salt and *patis* in a bowl. Stir well to blend flavors. Add freshly ground pepper. Let rest a few minutes then pour over tossed vegetables just before serving.

Serves 4–6
Preparation time: 15 mins

Escabeche
(Fried Fish with Sweet and Sour Sauce)

1 kg (2 lb) whole red snapper, cleaned
75 g ($^1/_2$ cup) plain flour, for dredging
125 ml ($^1/_2$ cup) oil
100 g ($^1/_2$ cup) caster sugar
125 ml($^1/_2$ cup) vinegar
125 ml ($^1/_2$ cup) water
3 tablespoons tomato ketchup
1 medium carrot, peeled and cut into 1-cm ($^1/_2$-in) rounds
1 medium green capsicum, cut into 1-cm ($^1/_2$-in) strips
1 medium red capsicum, cut into 1-cm ($^1/_2$-in) strips
1 medium cucumber, peeled and cut into 1-cm ($^1/_2$-in) rounds
Fresh coriander leaves (cilantro), to garnish

1 Score the red snapper all over and dredge in flour. Heat oil in a wok and fry the fish about 10 minutes on one side and 6 to 7 minutes on the other side, until completely cooked and fish flesh is no longer glassy. Remove from pan and drain on paper towels.
2 Combine sugar, vinegar, water and tomato ketchup in a saucepan. Add carrot, cook for about 5 minutes, then add capsicums and cucumber. Simmer, without stirring, for a further 5 minutes or until vegetables are tender yet firm.
3 Arrange fish on a serving platter. Pour vinegar mixture over fish. Arrange vegetables around fish and garnish with fresh coriander.

Serves 6
Preparation time: 15 mins
Cooking time: 25 mins

Rellenong Bangus (Stuffed Milkfish)

1 *bangus* (milkfish), about 700 g (1 1/3 lb)
4 *calamansi*
2 tablespoons soy sauce
2 tablespoons oil for sautéeing
1/2 medium onion, finely chopped
3–4 cloves garlic, peeled and diced
1 small potato, peeled, cubed small and fried to light brown
100 g (1/2 cup) green peas
90 g (1/2 cup) raisins
Worcestershire sauce
Salt and pepper
1 egg, lightly beaten
Cornstarch, for dredging
125 ml (1/2 cup) oil for deep-frying

Serves 4–6
Preparation time: **1 hour**
Cooking time: **40–50 mins**

1 Slit the fish and clean thoroughly. Scoop out the flesh, being careful not to tear the skin. Pick off all the bones from the bangus flesh. Set flesh aside. Marinate skin in juice of 3 of the *calamansi* and soy sauce. Set aside.

2 In a frying-pan, heat 2 tablespoons oil and sauté onion until soft. Add garlic and sauté until fragrant. Stir in *bangus* flesh and sauté until *bangus* is fully cooked. Add diced potato, peas and raisins. Season with a dash of Worcestershire sauce, salt and pepper and juice of remaining 1 *calamansi*. Stir well to mix. Remove from heat and mix in the egg.

3 Remove fish skin from marinade. Spoon the flesh mixture back into the skin but do not overstuff. Set aside any of the stuffings that won't fit into the *bangus*—this can be served separately. Sew the fish with a needle and thread to seal the stuffing in, then dredge *bangus* in cornstarch.

4 Heat the 125 ml oil in a wok or frying-pan. Fry the whole milkfish in hot oil until golden brown.

Scoop out the flesh, being careful not to tear the skin.

Marinate skin in calamansi juice.

Spoon the bangus flesh back into the skin.

Seal the bangus with a needle and thread.

Adobong Alimango
(Stewed Mud Crabs)

Be sure to buy mud crabs that are still alive. The vendors will usually tie the crab claws to prevent the crabs from escaping. Store live crabs in a container that allows them to breathe. Cook as soon as possible.

4 medium *alimango* (mud crabs)
60 ml ($^1/_4$ cup) oil
1 whole head garlic, cloves peeled and crushed
375 ml (1$^1/_2$ cups) water
80 ml ($^1/_3$ cup) *calamansi* juice
Salt and pepper

1 Cut the crabs into half. Remove the yellow crab fat and set this aside. Heat the oil in a wok and sauté garlic, about 1 minute. Add the crabs and stir until almost reddish in color.
2 Blend the reserved crab tissue with water and *calamansi* juice until smooth. Pour into the wok and season with salt and pepper. Simmer over medium heat until crabs are fully cooked, about 10 minutes.

Serves 4
Preparation time: **10 mins**
Cooking time: **15 mins**

Rellenong Alimasag (Stuffed Crabs)

Those who like the taste of crabs will enjoy eating this dish. The stuffing contains only pure crab meat, sautéed with garlic, onion and tomatoes, which give it added flavor. You may steam the crab ahead and pry the meat from the shells. Keep crab meat refrigerated until ready to cook as stuffing.

6 crabs
90 ml (¹/₃ cup) oil
1 small onion, diced
3–4 cloves garlic, peeled and diced
2–3 small tomatoes, diced
Salt and pepper
1 egg, lightly beaten
2 tablespoons cornstarch
2 tablespoons bread-crumbs

Serves 4–6
Preparation time: 10 mins
Cooking time: 30 mins

1 Steam crabs until fully cooked, about 10 minutes. Allow to cool. Open crabs and remove the meat from the crabs. Set the meat aside. Reserve shells and claws.
2 Heat 2 tablespoons of the oil in a frying-pan and sauté onion for 1 minute. Add garlic and sauté until fragrant. Add the tomatoes and sauté until tender. Stir in the crabmeat and mix well. Season with salt and pepper. Remove from heat.
3 Spoon crabmeat mixture back into each of the shells. Brush lightly with egg, then dust lightly with corn-starch and breadcrumbs.
4 Heat remaining oil in a pan and cook crab shells in the hot oil, stuffed side facing down, until a light brown crust is formed on the surface of the stuffed side. Remove from heat and serve with the reserved claws.

You may also remove the meat from the crab claws and sauté it with the rest of the crabmeat.

Chicken Cocido

This dish—of Spanish origin—has many versions. This recipe combines chicken with Spanish sausage (chorizo) and assorted vegetables to make a flavorful one-dish meal.

60 ml ($1/4$ cup) olive oil
2 chorizo sausages, sliced on the diagonal
1 medium onion, minced
$1/2$ head garlic, cloves peeled and crushed
1 kg (2 lb) whole chicken, cut into serving pieces
500 ml (2 cups) water
2 medium carrots, sliced into 1 cm ($1/2$ in) rounds
2 potatoes, peeled and quartered
2–3 *saba* bananas (plantains), sliced into 4-cm (2-in) diagonal pieces
500 ml (2 cups) canned tomato sauce
1 medium head of cabbage, quartered
Patis (fish sauce)
Calamansi juice to taste

1 In a large casserole, heat olive oil about 1 minute. Sauté the chorizo until firm, about 2 minutes on each side. Remove from heat and set aside. In same oil, sauté onion 1 to 2 minutes, then add garlic and sauté until fragrant. Add chicken and brown lightly. Pour in water, bring to the boil then lower heat and simmer for 10 minutes.

2 Add carrots, cook for about 8 minutes, then add potatoes, bananas and chorizo sausage.

3 Stir in tomato sauce and let mixture simmer until chicken, vegetables and bananas are almost tender. Add the cabbage and heat through until cabbage leaves are tender but crisp and chicken is completely cooked.

4 Serve with rice and a dip of *patis* and *calamansi*.

Serves 4–6
Preparation time: **15 mins**
Cooking time: **40–50 mins**

Chicken and Pork Adobo

500 g (1 lb) pork belly or pork shoulder, cut into
  large chunks
1 whole chicken, cut into serving pieces
1 head of garlic, cloves peeled and crushed
375 ml (1¹/₂ cups) cane or white vinegar
375 ml (1¹/₂ cups) water
1 bay leaf
500 g (1 lb) chicken livers
125 ml (¹/₂ cup) oil
60 ml (¹/₄ cup) soy sauce

1 Combine pork and chicken in a casserole. Sprinkle
garlic on top. In a bowl, mix vinegar and 250 ml (1 cup)
of the water. Pour over the pork and chicken then add
the bay leaf. Bring to the boil without stirring. When
the mixture boils, lower heat and simmer until pork
and chicken are tender, about 30 minutes. Remove
pork and chicken and set aside, reserve the liquid.
2 Meanwhile, simmer chicken livers in remaining
water until tender, about 10 minutes. Remove chicken
livers from water and pound lightly. Return pounded
livers to the water and mix well.
3 Heat the oil in a wok and fry the cooked pork and
chicken until brown. Stir in the reserved liquid and
the chicken liver mixture to thicken the sauce. Blend
in soy sauce and simmer for about 5 minutes. Remove
the bay leaf. Serve with rice or *pan de sal* or any type
of bread desired. Bread is good for sopping up the
sauce. Either serve immediately or set aside and reheat
before serving.

Serves 4–6
Preparation time: **10 mins**
Cooking time: **1¹/₂ hours**

Chicken Pastel
(Chicken Casserole Baked in a Crust)

1 whole chicken, about
  1 kg (2 lb), cut into
  bite-sized pieces
Juice of 4 *calamansi*
60 ml ($^1/_4$ cup) soy sauce
2 tablespoons olive oil
2 chorizo sausages, sliced
  on the diagonal about
  1 cm ($^1/_2$ in) thick
50 g ($^1/_4$ cup) butter
1 medium onion, diced
3–4 cloves garlic, peeled
  and diced
250 ml (1 cup) water
1 medium carrot, sliced
  into rounds
2 medium potatoes, cut
  into quarters
60 ml ($^1/_4$ cup) white
  wine
1 140 g (5 oz) tin Vienna
  sausage, cut into 1-cm
  ($^1/_2$-in) pieces
250 g (1 cup) button
  mushrooms
200 g (1 cup) green peas
Salt and pepper
2 tablespoons cornstarch
60 ml ($^1/_4$ cup) water
3 hard-boiled eggs
1 standard pie crust
1 egg yolk, lightly beaten

1 Marinate chicken in *calamansi* juice and soy sauce.
2 In a casserole, heat olive oil and sauté chorizo until firm, about 2 minutes on each side. Remove chorizo and set aside.
3 Add butter to casserole. When butter melts, sauté onion until transparent, 1 to 2 minutes. Add garlic and sauté until fragrant. Add the chicken (discarding the marinade) and brown.
4 Stir in water and simmer over low heat for about 10 minutes. Add carrot and potatoes and simmer until chicken, carrot and potatoes are almost tender, about 15 minutes. Stir in white wine, sausage, mushrooms, peas and the cooked chorizo. Season with salt and pepper.
5 Preheat oven to 190°C (375°F). In a small bowl, blend cornstarch and water until smooth and stir into casserole. Simmer until liquid thickens, about 5 minutes.
6 Spoon mixture into a baking dish. Slice hard-boiled eggs and place on top of mixture. Cover baking dish with the pie crust and brush the crust with egg yolk. Make slits on surface of the crust to let steam escape. Bake for about 30 minutes or until crust is golden brown.

Serves 6–8
Preparation time: 30 mins + time for making pie crust
Cooking time: 1 hour 10 mins

Morcon (Stuffed Beef Roll)

1½ kg (3 lb) top round beef cut into one whole sheet about ½ cm (¼ in) thick (have your butcher do this for you)
Juice of 5–6 *calamansi*
60 ml (¼ cup) soy sauce
1–2 pork or beef frankfurters (hot dogs)
1–2 whole sweet pickles (or gerkins as substitute)
1–2 hard-boiled eggs, sliced vertically
1 medium carrot, sliced into 1-cm (½-in) strips
Flour for dusting
60 ml (¼ cup) oil
250 ml (1 cup) water
2 medium tomatoes, seeded and chopped
1 bay leaf
Salt and pepper to taste

Serves 4–6
Preparation time: **45 mins**
Cooking time: **1½ hours**

1 Marinate beef in a mixture of *calamansi* juice and soy sauce for about 30 minutes. Drain beef and reserve marinade.
2 Spread beef on a clean, dry surface such as a cookie sheet or jelly roll pan. If the sheet of beef is too long, divide in the middle. On each sheet of beef arrange, in a row, 1 frankfurter, 1 whole pickle, some egg slices and 1 or 2 carrot strips. Roll beef, enclosing the fillings. Tie with a string.
3 Dust rolled beef lightly with flour. In a casserole, heat cooking oil and brown the tied beef on all sides. Pour in water, tomatoes and reserved marinade. Simmer over low heat until beef is fully cooked and tender, about 1 to 1½ hours. Make sure the water does not dry up—add more if necessary.
4 Remove beef from casserole and reserve the liquid. Let cool a few minutes then slice into serving pieces. Discard the strings.
5 Strain the liquid and serve as sauce for the beef.

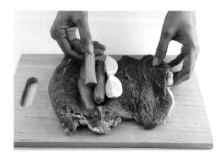

Place the items in a line in the center of the beef.

Roll the beef and tie with string.

Kare-Kare (Oxtail in Peanut-flavored Stew)

1 kg (2 lb) oxtail, sliced
1 kg (2 lb) ox leg, sliced
1 $^1/_2$ liters (6 cups) water
  for first boiling
3 liters (12 cups) water
  for second boiling
2 tablespoons oil
1 medium onion, diced
3–4 cloves garlic, peeled
  and diced
100 g (2 slices) heart of
  banana, sliced into
  1-cm ($^1/_2$-in) pieces
  (optional)
1 medium eggplant,
  sliced diagonally into
  1-cm ($^1/_2$-in) pieces
100 g (1 cup) *sitaw*
  (snake beans), cut into
  4 cm-(1$^3/_4$-in) lengths
2 tablespoons annatto
  seeds
$^1/_2$ cup toasted peanuts,
  finely ground (see Note)
$^1/_2$ cup toasted raw rice,
  finely pounded (see
  Note)
1 tablespoon *bagoong*
  (shrimp paste)

Serves 8
Preparation time: 30 mins
Cooking time: 2 hours

1 Clean oxtail and ox leg thoroughly, removing any remaining dirt. In a stockpot, boil the oxtail and ox leg in 1$^1/_2$ liters (6 cups) water for about 10 minutes. Drain and discard the water. Return the oxtail and ox leg into the stockpot and pour in 3 liters (12 cups) water. Bring to the boil then simmer over low heat until meats are tender, about 1$^1/_2$ hours.
2 Remove meats from broth and reserve broth. Slice the meats from the bones. Discard bones and set meats aside.
3 In a casserole, heat oil and sauté onion for 1 minute, or until transparent. Add garlic and sauté 1 more minute. Pour in 1 liter (4 cups) of the reserved broth. Add the heart of banana if using, bring to the boil and simmer for about 5 minutes or until almost tender. Add the eggplant and *sitaw* and simmer until almost tender.
4 Soak the annatto seeds in 60 ml ($^1/_4$ cup) of the reserved broth. Strain the liquid, pour into casserole and mix well. Stir in the ground peanuts and pounded rice grains to thicken the liquid then add the tenderized meats.
5 Blend *bagoong* with 60 ml ($^1/_4$ cup) of the remaining broth and pour into casserole. Simmer for a further 5 minutes or until heated through. Serve with rice and additional *bagoong*.

Toast the raw peanuts (or rice) over medium heat, stirring continuously until brown all over. Pound finely in a mortar and pestle or grind in a food processor.

Mechado
(Beef Stewed in Beer and Tomato Sauce)

60 ml (¹/₄ cup) corn oil
1¹/₂ kg (3 lb) beef top round, rolled, and tied with 500 g (1 lb) pork fat inserted (have your butcher do this for you)
1 medium onion, sliced
2–3 cloves garlic, peeled and crushed
2 tins (3 cups) chopped tomatoes
60 ml (¹/₄ cup) soy sauce
60 ml (¹/₄ cup) *calamansi* juice
250 ml (1 cup) water
2 bay leaves
2 medium potatoes, peeled and quartered
250 ml (1 cup) beer
2 medium carrots, cut into 1-cm (¹/₂-in) rounds

1 Heat oil in a casserole or braising pan. Add the beef and brown all sides. Remove meat and set aside.
2 In the same casserole, sauté onion about 1 minute. Add garlic and sauté until fragrant but not brown. Mix tomatoes, soy sauce, *calamansi* and water in a bowl, then pour into the casserole.
3 Return beef to casserole and add bay leaves. Bring to the boil, then reduce to medium heat and simmer, covered, for about 1 hour. After 1 hour, add potatoes, beer and carrots. Continue simmering until potatoes, beef and carrots are tender, about 20 more minutes. By this time, the sauce will have thickened slightly.
4 Remove from heat and discard bay leaves. Let beef rest for a few minutes, then slice into serving pieces and serve with the sauce.

Serves 8–10
Preparation time: **15 mins**
Cooking time: **1¹/₂ hours**

Insert pork fat into the beef.

Roll up the beef and tie with string.

Inihaw na Baboy
(Grilled Marinated Pork)

1 head garlic, cloves peeled and crushed
250 ml (1 cup) 7-Up or Sprite
100 g ($^1/_2$ cup) brown sugar
1 kg (2 lb) pork belly, sliced lengthwise about
  2 cm ($^3/_4$ in) wide

Dip
1 head garlic, peeled and crushed
250 ml (1 cup) vinegar
125 ml ($^1/_2$ cup) soy sauce
Freshly ground pepper

1 Combine the garlic, 7-Up or Sprite, and brown sugar in a bowl. Add the pork, stir and marinate for 2 to 4 hours.
2 When ready to cook, drain pork and discard the marinade. Heat grill to medium and grill pork, turning occasionally, until thoroughly cooked.
3 To make the dip, combine garlic, vinegar and soy sauce. Season with pepper to taste.
4 Serve the grilled pork with the dip and cooked white rice.

Serves 4–6
Preparation time: **10 mins + 2–4 hours marinating**
Cooking time: **30 mins**

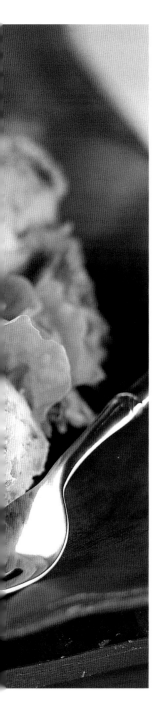

Embutido
(Filipino Meat Loaf)

1 slice white bread with crust
60 ml ($^1/_4$ cup) fresh or evaporated milk
400 g (2$^1/_2$ cups) ground pork
1 140 g (5 oz) tin Vienna sausage, chopped
2 pieces chorizo sausage, chopped
100 g (1$^1/_2$ cups) raisins
200 ml ($^3/_4$ cup) sweet pickle relish
4 eggs
$^1/_2$ cup crushed pineapple
Salt and pepper to taste
Butter for greasing
4 hard-boiled eggs, sliced crosswise

1 Soak bread in milk for a few minutes. In a large mixing bowl, combine the bread, ground pork, sausage, chorizo, raisins, pickle relish, 4 eggs and crushed pineapple. Mix well by hand. Season with salt and pepper.
2 Cut 4 pieces of foil about 30 x 45 cm (1 x 1$^1/_2$ ft). Brush butter on foil and spread about one quarter of the pork mixture on each foil. Arrange slices of hard boiled egg on each pork mixture.
3 Roll pork into a log, using the edge of the foil to help in the rolling process. Wrap tightly with the foil and seal the edges.
4 Steam the pork rolls in a steamer about 40 minutes or until firm.

The meat loaf can be cooked ahead and refrigerated. It can be served hot with rice or cold as filling for a sandwich. As it should be sliced before serving, you may want to chill it slightly so it doesn't crumble when cutting. After slicing, warm the embutido in the microwave or non-stick pan if desired.

Makes 4 rolls
Preparation time: 30 mins
Cooking time: 40 mins

Callos (Tripe and Sausage with Chickpeas)

500 g (1 lb) ox tripe
500 ml (2 cups) vinegar
7 liters (28 cups) water
750 g (1$^1/_2$ lb) ox hooves
2 tablespoons corn oil
2 chorizo sausages, sliced
  diagonally into 1-cm
  ($^1/_2$-in) pieces
60 ml ($^1/_4$ cup) extra
  virgin olive oil
1 small onion, diced
3–4 cloves garlic, peeled
  and crushed
250 ml (1 cup) chopped
  tomatoes (fresh or
  canned)
375 ml (1$^1/_2$ cups)
  canned tomato sauce
1 medium red capsicum,
  cut into 2$^1/_2$-cm (1-in)
  squares
85 g ($^2/_3$ cup) pitted
  green olives
100 g ($^3/_4$ cup) chickpeas
Salt and pepper
Tabasco sauce (optional)

Serves 8–10
Preparation time: 50 mins
Cooking time: 2$^1/_2$ hours

1 Wash ox tripe in vinegar thoroughly. Rinse and brush to remove any dirt. Boil tripe in 2 liters (8 cups) of the water for 10 minutes. Drain and discard water.
2 Wash ox hooves well. Boil in 2 liters (8 cups) of the water for 10 minutes. Drain and discard water.
3 In a stockpot, combine ox tripe and ox hooves. Pour in remaining 3 liters (12 cups) water and bring to the boil, then simmer for about 2 hours or until meats are tender. Remove meats from broth and let cool. Reserve 375 ml (1$^1/_2$ cups) of the broth.
4 Meanwhile, heat corn oil in a frying-pan and fry the chorizo pieces until firm, about 2 to 3 minutes per side. Set aside.
5 Slice the tripe into 2-cm (1-in) squares. Remove meat from the ox hooves and slice similarly. Set aside.
6 Heat olive oil in a casserole and sauté onion until transparent. Add garlic and sauté until fragrant. Add the sliced meats and sauté until lightly brown. Pour in tomatoes, canned tomato sauce and the reserved broth. Simmer for about 5 minutes.
7 Add the chorizo, capsicum, olives and chickpeas and season with salt, pepper and, if desired Tabasco. Simmer just enough for the vegetables to heat through.

Pochero (Beef Shanks with Vegetables)

3–4 ripe *saba* bananas (plantains)

2 tablespoons oil

2 pieces chorizo sliced into 1-cm ($^1/_2$-in) pieces

1 kg (2 lb) boneless beef shanks

2 liters (8 cups) beef stock

2 medium potatoes, peeled and quartered

100 g ($^3/_4$ cup) chickpeas

1 cabbage, quartered

2 tablespoons *patis* (fish sauce)

Dip

250 ml (1 cup) *patis* (fish sauce)

125 ml ($^1/_2$ cup) *calamansi* juice

1 Peel then slice the *saba* bananas diagonally into $2^1/_2$-cm (1-in) pieces and set aside.

2 In a frying-pan, heat oil and fry the chorizo about 2 minutes on each side or until firm. Set aside.

3 In a stockpot, bring the beef shanks and beef stock to the boil, then lower heat and simmer for about $1^1/_2$ hours, or until beef is almost tender. Add water if necessary to make sure it does not dry out.

4 Add the potatoes and the bananas. Simmer for about 15 minutes more, then add the chickpeas and chorizo and continue simmering for another 5 minutes.

5 Add the cabbage and season with *patis*. Simmer just until cabbage is tender crisp, about 2 to 3 minutes.

6 To make the Dip, blend ingredients then divide into individual portions. Serve Pochero with rice and Dip.

Serves 6–8
Preparation time: **15 mins**
Cooking time: **2 hours**

Humba (Stewed Pork)

100 g ($^{1}/_{2}$ cup) brown
  sugar
500 ml (2 cups) water
60 ml ($^{1}/_{4}$ cup) soy sauce
200 ml (scant $^{3}/_{4}$ cup)
  vinegar
1 kg (2 lb) pork shoulder,
  cut into large chunks
3–4 cloves garlic, peeled
  and crushed
1 bay leaf

1 Combine sugar, water, soy sauce, and vinegar in a
bowl and stir well. Transfer to a casserole and add the
pork chunks, garlic and bay leaf.
2 Bring to the boil, then lower heat to simmer. Simmer
over low heat until pork is tender, about 35 minutes.
3 Discard bay leaf and serve meat with rice. Spoon
over the sauce.

Serves 6
Preparation time: 5 mins
Cooking time: 40 mins

Caldereta (Rich Beef Stew)

This dish is a favorite at town fiestas. Long, slow simmering makes the beef tender, while the chorizo, peas and olives add richness to the taste.

60 ml ($^1/_4$ cup) olive oil
1 kg (2 lb) stewing beef, cut into chunks
1 medium onion, sliced lengthwise
$1^1/_2$ liters (6 cups) water
500 g (1 lb) pork liver
2 chorizo sausages, sliced diagonally into $2^1/_2$-cm (1-in) pieces
$1^1/_2$ heads garlic, cloves peeled and chopped
330 ml ($1^1/_3$ cups) canned tomato sauce
80 ml ($^1/_3$ cup) white vinegar
240 g (1 cup) grated Cheddar cheese
2 tablespoons white granulated sugar
Salt and pepper to taste
2 medium potatoes, peeled and quartered
2 medium carrots, sliced into $2^1/_2$-cm (1-in) rounds
1 red capsicum, sliced lengthwise in $2^1/_2$-cm (1-in) slices
200 g ($1^1/_2$ cups) green peas
100 g ($^1/_2$ cup) sliced green or black olives

1 In a large casserole, heat 2 tablespoons of the olive oil and brown beef on all sides. Transfer beef and olive oil to a stockpot. Add the onion to the beef and pour in water. Bring to the boil, then lower the heat and simmer.

2 Meanwhile, grill pork liver until it is half cooked, about 5 to 10 minutes. Chop finely.

3 In a large saucepan, heat remaining oil and sauté the chorizo until firm, about 2 minutes per side. Remove from pan and set aside. In same oil sauté garlic until fragrant. Stir in the chopped liver, tomato sauce and vinegar. Add the cheese, sugar, salt and pepper. Mix well and simmer 5 minutes, stirring occasionally, until mixture is smooth.

4 Pour this liver and cheese mixture into the simmering beef in the casserole. Stir to combine mixture well with the liquid. Allow beef to continue simmering for about 30 minutes.

5 Add potatoes and carrots and simmer until beef, potatoes and carrots are tender and sauce has thickened, about 30 more minutes.

6 Stir in cooked chorizo, capsicum, green peas and olives. Heat through. Serve with rice.

Serves 6–8
Preparation time: **15 mins**
Cooking time: **1 hour 30 mins**

Mechadong Dila (Ox Tongue Casserole)

1¹/₂ kg (3 lb) ox tongue
4 liters (16 cups) water
1 onion, sliced
2 tablespoons olive oil
4 cloves garlic, peeled
  and crushed
500 g (3 cups) chopped
  tomatoes with juice
200 ml (scant ³/₄ cup)
  canned tomato sauce
125 ml (¹/₂ cup)
  calamansi juice
60 ml (¹/₄ cup) soy
  sauce
2 medium potatoes,
  quartered
1 medium carrot, cut into
  1 cm (¹/₂ in) rounds
Sliced olives (optional)

1 Bring ox tongue and 2 liters (8 cups) of the water in to the boil in a stockpot. Reduce the heat and simmer about 20 minutes until a white coating appears on the ox tongue. Remove ox tongue from water and scrape off the white coating. Discard the water.

2 Return ox tongue to stockpot and pour in remaining 2 liters (8 cups) water. Add onion, bring to the boil, then simmer until ox tongue is almost tender, about 1 hour. Remove ox tongue from stockpot and refrigerate for about 2 hours to firm it up, so it does not crumble when sliced. Reserve the stock.

3 Slice ox tongue into serving pieces. Heat olive oil in a large casserole and sauté the garlic about 1 minute. Pour in chopped tomatoes, their juices as well as the canned tomato sauce and two cups of the reserved stock. Add the sliced ox tongue. Bring to a simmer, then stir in *calamansi* juice and soy sauce.

4 Add potatoes, carrot and olives, if using, then let mixture simmer until ox tongue, potatoes and carrot are fork tender, about 30 more minutes.

Serves 6–8
Preparation time: 30 mins + 2 hours refrigeration time
Cooking time: 1¹/₂ hours

Leche Flan (Créme Caramel)

150 g (1 cup) brown
sugar
60 ml ($^1/_4$ cup) water
6 eggs + 2 extra yolks
300 g (1$^1/_2$ cups) white
granulated sugar
375 ml (1$^1/_2$ cups)
evaporated milk
Zest of 1 *dayap* (key
lime), or 1 lemon
or lime

1 To make the caramel base, combine brown sugar and water in a saucepan. Allow sugar to melt over low heat until a syrup forms. Pour immediately into two *llaneras* or one loaf tin. Tilt pan(s) to make sure syrup coats bottoms of pans evenly. Set aside.

2 Lightly beat the whole eggs and extra egg yolks in a mixing bowl. Add sugar and evaporated milk and stir to mix. Strain into prepared pan(s), then stir in the *dayap* zest.

3 Cover pan(s) with foil and place in a steamer and cook for 50 minutes to 1 hour or until Leche Flan is firm to the touch. Let it cool. Chill 3 to 4 hours or refrigerate overnight before serving.

4 To serve, run a spatula or knife along the edge of the pan to loosen the flan. Turn out onto a serving platter.

Serves 4
Preparation time: **15 mins + 3–4 hours refrigeration time**
Cooking time: **1 hour**

Haleyang Ube (Purple Yam Pudding)

Sweet and sticky, this dessert makes good use of *ube*, or purple yam. *Ube* is also a favorite ingredient in the popular iced dessert Halo-Halo and in ice-cream.

2 kg (4 lb) fresh *ube* (purple yam)
375 ml (1 1/2 cups) evaporated milk
600 ml (2 1/3 cups) sweetened condensed milk
200 g (1 cup) white granulated sugar
Kaong (palm nut) (optional)

Serves 6–8
Preparation time: **30 mins**
Cooking time: **30 mins**

1 Cover the yam with water and bring to the boil over medium heat to cook until tender. Peel then mash the yam finely with a potato masher.

2 Put the mashed yam in a heavy pan or wok. Pour in the evaporated milk and condensed milk. Add the sugar. Simmer gently over low heat, stirring continuously with a wooden or chef's spoon, for 30 minutes. Make sure the bottom does not scorch.

3 Cook until mixture becomes thick, and takes effort to stir.

4 Spoon into clean containers and cool. Do not cover containers while yam is still hot as this can spoil it.

5 Serve warm or cold as dessert. Top with *kaong*, if desired.

Halo-Halo (Iced Fruit Mix)

The literal translation of halo halo is "mix-mix". This iced dessert is a melange of sweet fruits, beans, tapioca, leche flan and ube jam, served with crushed ice, milk and sugar in a tall glass. Like a parfait, it yields a variety of flavors with every spoonful. Use as many or as few as you like of each ingredient listed.

6 ripe *saba* bananas (plaintains)
1 liter (4 cups) bottled sweetened red *mongo* (mung) beans, drained to yield 4 cups
1 liter (4 cups) bottled sweetened white beans, drained to yield 4 cups
1 liter (4 cups) bottled sweetened jackfruit, drained to yield 3 cups
1 liter (4 cups) bottled sweetened *kaong* (palm nut), drained to yield 3 cups
1 cup cooked sago (tapioca pearls)
200 g (1 cup) caster sugar
Crushed ice
750 ml (3 cups) fresh milk
24 oz bottle (4 cups) *ube* (yam) jam
6 slices leche flan (créme caramel, see page 58), cut into squares
$^1/_2$ cup *pinipig* (substitute Rice Krispies breakfast cereal)
6 scoops of ice-cream (any flavor)

1 Boil bananas about 10 mins or until tender. Peel and slice into 2 cm (1in) pieces. Set aside to cool.
2 Divide the bananas, *mongo* beans, white beans, jackfruit, *kaong* and sago into 6 tall parfait glasses, the proportion of the ingredients depending on one's own preference. Add sugar to taste.
3 Fill the glasses with crushed ice. Pour about 125 ml ($^1/_2$ cup) milk into each glass. Spoon *ube*, leche flan and *pinipig* on top of the crushed ice. Top each glass with a scoop of ice cream. Serve with long-handled spoons.

The bottled ingredients are widely available from Filipino grocers.

Serves 6
Preparation time: **20–30 mins**

Maja Blanca (Coconut Milk Pudding)

200 ml (³/₄ cup) water
1 kg (2 lb) fresh grated
   coconut
1¹/₂ cups corn kernels,
   drained
200 g (1 cup) caster
   sugar
200 g (1 cup) *galapong*
   (rice flour), substitute
   with cornflour
1 liter (4 cups) fresh or
   canned coconut milk

Serves 8
Preparation time: **40 mins**
Cooking time: **1 hour**

1 Add the water to the grated coconut. Squeeze to extract coconut milk. Strain coconut milk into a pan and heat over moderate heat, stirring occasionally, about 20 to 25 minutes. If mixture becomes too thick, add 60 ml (¹/₄ cup) water. The mixture will brown, become oily and, after a while, it will clump together and turn into brown granules. Continue stirring. The granules are known as *latik*, which is used as a topping for the dish. Strain the oil into a bowl and set aside both the coconut oil and the *latik*.
2 Combine corn, sugar, rice flour and coconut milk in a large casserole or wok. Cook over moderate heat, stirring constantly until mixture begins to thicken. Add the strained coconut oil, a little at a time, to prevent the mixture from sticking to the pan. Continue stirring until mixture thickens.
3 Pour into a container (a Pyrex dish will do). Set aside until mixture becomes solid, about 2 to 3 hours. Sprinkle all the *latik* on top. Cut into slices and serve warm or at room temperature.

Matamis na Saging
(Sweetened Bananas Cooked in Syrup)

Saba bananas are similar to plantain. In this dessert, which can be served warm or cold, they are sweetened in syrup. Either way, this is a satisfying meal ender.

1 kg (2 lb) ripe *saba* bananas (plaintains)
400 g (2 cups) brown sugar
1 liter (4 cups) water
375 ml (1¹/₂ cups) milk (optional)

Serves 6
Preparation time: **5 mins**
Cooking time: **50 mins**

1 Peel the bananas, then slice each banana on the diagonal into three pieces.
2 In a large saucepan, combine sugar and water. Bring to the boil, stirring occasionally, until sugar dissolves. Add the bananas and return to the boil. Lower the heat immediately to a simmer. Skim off any scum (impurities) that rise to the surface and discard.
3 Simmer until bananas are tender and liquid reduces to a thick, syrupy consistency, about 40 minutes.
4 Divide into 6 serving bowls and serve warm or cold with crushed ice. Add about 60 ml ($^1/_4$ cup) milk to each bowl if desired.

Index